Comprehension Success

Success

4

James Driver

Oxford University Press

Preface

Comprehension is a comprehensive activity that involves many different aspects of English. This book uses the traditional role of comprehension – asking questions on the content of short texts - as a starting-point from which to investigate, in depth, a variety of different kinds of writing.

The thirty double-pages of comprehensions offer a wide variety of texts – examples from information books, action rhymes, realia such as postcards and notices, children's fiction, fable, catalogues, comic strips, picture books, poems and legends – a whole range of genres, drawn from authentic texts.

The pupils are then encouraged to use a range of strategies to discover meaning. They will practise locating, selecting, collating, identifying, using, retrieving, examining and re-presenting ideas and information, and, by employing quotation, deduction and inference, find that their confidence as readers who fully appreciate a text will continue to grow.

There are three sections on most of the question pages. Section A contains the most straightforward recall questions. The questions in Section B often call for a deeper insight into the nature of the text. The knowledge gained from answering one, or both, of these two sets of questions is used in Section C, which offers a prompt for a creative writing activity, in the same genre as the selected text.

The confidence that comes from being able to understand the main points about the facts, characters and events that appear in a broad range of texts encourages readers to read more widely and enables them to gain a better understanding of how writing, its form, language and content, works. This, in turn, should lead to a faster development of their ability as writers.

Oxford University Press, Great Clarendon Street, Oxford OX2 6DP

Oxford New York
Athens Auckland Bangkok Bogota Bombay
Buenos Aires Calcutta Cape Town Dar es Salaam
Delhi Florence Hong Kong Istanbul Karachi
Kuala Lumpur Madras Madrid Melbourne
Mexico City Nairobi Paris Singapore
Taipei Tokyo Toronto Warsaw

and associated companies in
Berlin Ibadan

Oxford is a trade mark of Oxford University Press

© Oxford University Press 1998
First published 1998

ISBN 0 19 834181 4

Typeset and designed by Oxprint Design, Oxford

Printed in Hong Kong

Contents

Books and authors

Here are some facts about *three authors* and some facts about *three books*, all taken from cover blurbs for the Treetops series.

About the author

Sylvia Moody

I am a writer and translator of children's books and I also work with children and adults who find reading difficult.

I was born in Yorkshire and after college, I went to work in Greece for fifteen years. I lived in a little castle on the Island of Crete where there were three enormous dogs.

Now I live in London in a very quiet street and that is what gave me the idea for this story...

About the author

Roger Stevens

I was a teacher in a Primary School but I really wanted to write. It took a lot of stories and poems before my first book was published.

I live in Faversham with my wife Jill, who is a journalist. Between us we have three children, Paul, Kate and Joseph. I also play in a band and I am half of the travelling Poetry Road Show.

When I first told this story, a teacher called Mrs Moss thought I must have made it up about her. I hadn't. But that goes to show that stories can be just like real life.

About the author

Paul Shipton

When I was growing up in Manchester, I always wanted to be an astronaut, a footballer, or (if those didn't work out for any reason) perhaps a rock star. So it came as something of a shock when I became first a teacher and then an editor of educational books.

I have lived in Cambridge, Aylesbury, Oxford and Istanbul. I'm still on the run and now live in Chicago with my wife Vicky and daughter Megan.

Most of the characters in this book are animals that I have known at one time or another.

PET SQUAD

Have you ever wondered who looks after your pets when humans aren't around? The answer might just be the Pet Squad – and their fearless leader, Bubbles the goldfish.

CALL 999!

'Egg and chips *and* fish fingers,' says Carla crossly to Jack and Kate. And this starts a string of disasters which shatter the peace of sleepy Church Lane. Will their neighbours ever get over it?

FRONT PAGE STORY

Sam and Lisa are reporters on their class newspaper. But what can they write about?

Then ten pounds goes missing and the two friends are on the trail of a mystery that really makes the front page.

1 a) Who do you think wrote *Call 999*?
  b) Give a good reason that explains why you think this particular author wrote this particular book.

2 a) Who do you think wrote *Pet Squad*?
  b) Give a good reason that explains why you think this particular author wrote this particular book.

3 a) Which one of the three authors would you ask to write a story about a footballer who travels with the England Team to play in the World Cup in America?
  b) Give **two** reasons why you would choose this particular author to write this particular book.

4 a) Which one of the three books is set in a school?
  b) Give a good reason for why you think the author of this book would be able to give an accurate picture of school life.

1 a) Which one of the three authors do you think has led the most exciting life?
  b) Give **two** good reasons why you chose this particular author.

2 You have to put these three books on the correct shelves in the school library.
  a) Which book would you put on the shelf labelled "**Crime**"?
  b) Give a good reason to explain why you chose to put this book there.

3 What advice do you think **Roger Stevens** would give you if you asked how to become a writer?

4 Why do you think **Bubbles** might find it difficult to be the leader of the Pet Squad?

Choose a book that you've enjoyed reading, and write a cover blurb to persuade your friends they'd like to read it.

August 1981

This page comes from a book which lists everything that happened in a particular year.

Thursday *August 20*	Officials announce delay of the second launch of the US space shuttle *Columbia* (due on September 30) because of complications with the rocket boosters.
Friday *August 21*	More than 100 dinosaur footprints have been found on a building site between 2 houses in Swanage, Dorset, 400m from the sea. Experts say they were made by *Meglosauruses*.
Saturday *August 22*	Julian Nott becomes the first person to cross the Channel in a solar-powered balloon: he takes 75 minutes to cross from South Barham, nr. Canterbury, to St. Inglevert, nr. Calais.
Sunday *August 23*	Europe's biggest marathon, with 8700 runners, from Bolton to Manchester and back, is won by Stanley Curran from Middleton, nr. Manchester. His time: 2 hrs, 19 mins. It's also his thirty-fourth birthday!
Monday *August 24*	Exhibition at the Commonwealth Institute includes the third largest star sapphire in the world. It is guarded by a cobra in the same showcase!
Tuesday *August 25*	*Voyager 2* approaches Saturn: it records a series of strange hums and whistles that are emitted by Saturn's rings and moons.
Wednesday *August 26*	*Voyager 2* is at its closest to Saturn (101,388.4 km). It sends back pictures of Hyperion, the eighth largest of Saturn's seventeen known moons—it looks like a battered potato! Steve Ovett wins back the mile record from Sebastian Coe in Koblenz with a time of 3 mins 48.40 secs.
Thursday *August 27*	Anne-France Rix (8) from Upper Poppleton nr. York, is the youngest winner of the Post Office's 1981 National Letter Writing Competition.
Friday *August 28*	Sebastian Coe takes the mile record back from Steve Ovett again in Brussels, with a time of 3 mins 47.33 secs.
Saturday *August 29*	Twenty-eight yachts leave Portsmouth at the start of the 41,842km Round-the-World Yacht Race. New Moon
Sunday *August 30*	Celebrity teddy bears attend the Bears' Bank Holiday at Longleat in Wiltshire. *Winnie the Pooh* is read in Latin. Mrs. Thatcher's teddy bear wears blue dungarees.
Monday *August 31*	Bank Holiday. DO NOT DISTURB notices outside Ching Ching's cage at London Zoo. She is believed to be pregnant and the crowds are gathering.

A

1 Why did Anne-France Rix win a prize?

2 How did Julian Nott travel to France?

3 Write down **two** facts the opposite page tells you about Saturn.

4 What would have happened to you if you had tried to steal the largest star sapphire in the world?

5 What sport was Steve Ovett involved in?

6 Who ran the longer distance in August, Sebastian Coe or Stanley Curran?

B

1 a) What do *Columbia* and *Voyager* have in common?
   b) Which one was working properly in August?
   c) Where was it on August 26th?

2 Where do you think the yachts leaving Portsmouth on August 29th will end their race? (Think **carefully**!)

3 a) List **three** methods of transport that are mentioned on the opposite page.
   b) Choose **one** of these methods of transport and explain why you would like to travel that way.

4 How can you tell that Ching Ching is a very rare animal?

C

The opposite page is from a **chronicle**. A **chronicle** has a date for every day of the year. Against each date there is a short passage that tells you about something that happened on that day in the past.

The most interesting chronicles are those that contain a mixture of events. The chronicle on the opposite page includes sport, birthdays, unusual events and news stories.

Make a **chronicle** of your own. List the days and dates for the last week. Try to include as many different events as you can. You might want to include things that have happened at school and at home as well as stories from television news, the radio and newspapers.

Old street cries

Two hundred years ago, street traders used to call out these verses, to persuade people to buy their wares.

SIXPENCE A POTTLE, FINE STRAWBERRIES!

'Strawberries, sixpence a pottle! So nice,
That surely you will not begrudge, Sir, the price;
Of treat more delicious could epicure dream,
Than these fine large strawberries with sugar
　　and cream?'

NEWS! GREAT NEWS IN THE LONDON GAZETTE!

'News! News! Here's great news in the London Gazette,
But what 'tis about, that I choose to forget—
For were I to speak all the news that befell,
I'm sure not a London Gazette could I sell!'

FLOUNDERS! JUMPING ALIVE! FINE FLOUNDERS!

'Come buy my live flounders! All jumping, ho!'
'Alive?' 'Yes, all jumping, Ma'am, two hours ago;
From sea just arrived, else may truth never thrive!
Fine flounders! Fresh flounders! all jumping alive!'

MATCHES! PLEASE TO WANT ANY MATCHES, MA'AM?

'Please want any matches, Ma'am?'—meekly and mild,
In piteous plaint ask poor woman and child;
'Do, Ma'am, buy a ha'p'orth of matches, pray do,
And blessing the poor, Ma'am, so will Heaven
　　bless you.'

LAMBS TO SELL! YOUNG LAMBS TO SELL!

A flock of young lambs, each so pretty and small,
This man in his basket can carry them all,
Save one on his finger, his business to tell,
While merrily singing, 'Young lambs to sell.'

CURRANTS, RED AND WHITE, A PENNY A PINT!

'Red and white currants, your thirst to allay,
Refreshingly cool on a warm summer day.
A penny a pint! Then come taste them, and try
My red and white currants! Come buy, come buy!'

A

1 List **two** different foods that the people in the pictures are selling.

2 List **two** different ways the street sellers carry the things they are selling.

3 What sort of toy could you buy on the streets of London?

4 What is the name of the newspaper the man is selling?

5 How, according to the woman who is selling them, can the currants help you on a very hot day?

B

1 Why does the man selling the newspaper say he has forgotten all the news that is in the newspaper?

2 Why does the man selling the flounders - which are a type of fish - tell his customers they are jumping about?

3 Write down the words used in the description of the lamb-seller that show he was happy.

4 **a)** Which one of the different things would **you** like to sell?
   b) Give a good reason to explain why you chose this one.

5 **a)** Which one of the sellers do you think has the hardest job?
   b) Give a good reason to explain why you chose this one.

C

The verses about the street sellers follow a pattern.
Each verse has four lines.
Line 1 in each verse rhymes with line 2.
Line 3 in each verse rhymes with line 4.
Most of the lines have 11 **syllables**, or beats in their metre.

Using the same pattern write a **verse** for a modern street seller who is selling computer games.

From stump to subway

This page is taken from the *Oxford Illustrated Junior Dictionary*.

stump *noun* **stumps**
1 the part of a broken tree, tooth, or pencil that is left.
2 one of the set of three upright sticks put at each end of the pitch in cricket.

stump 1

stun *verb* **stuns, stunning, stunned**
1 to hit or hurt someone so much that they cannot think properly.
2 to make someone very surprised. *She was stunned to receive so many presents.*

stung *verb* see **sting**

stunk *verb* see **stink**

stunt *noun* **stunts**
something difficult or dangerous done as part of a film or to attract people's attention.

stupid *adjective*
1 very silly. *a stupid idea.*
2 slow to learn and understand. *a stupid person.*
stupidly *adverb*

sturdy *adjective* **sturdier, sturdiest**
strong; not easily broken.
sturdy shoes.

stutter *verb* **stutters, stuttering, stuttered**
to keep repeating the sounds at the beginning of words when you speak.

sty *noun* **sties**
1 a sore swelling on the edge of an eyelid.
2 a place where pigs are kept.

style *noun* **styles**
the way something is done or made. *a neat style of writing, a hairstyle.*

subject *noun* **subjects**
1 the person or thing that you are writing about or learning about.
2 the subject of a sentence is the person or thing that does the action of the verb. In the sentence *Sam threw the ball*, *Sam* is the subject.
3 someone who is ruled by a king, queen, or government.

submarine *noun* **submarines**
a ship that can travel under water.

submit *verb* **submits, submitting, submitted**
1 to surrender.
2 to give something in to someone. *We must submit our work tomorrow.*

subscription *noun* **subscriptions**
money you pay regularly – for example, to belong to a club, or to get the same magazine each month.

substance *noun* **substances**
anything that you can see, touch, or use for making things. *Glue is a sticky substance.*

substitute *noun* **substitutes**
a person or thing used instead of the proper person or thing. *Our goalkeeper was ill, so we found a substitute.*

subtract *verb* **subtracts, subtracting, subtracted**
to take away. If you subtract 6 from 9 you get 3.
subtraction *noun* **subtractions**

subway *noun* **subways**
a tunnel made under the ground so that people can get to the other side of a road safely.

a b c d e f g h i j k l m n o p q r **s** t u v w x y z

A Fill in the gaps in these 5 questions by using any of the words that are printed in red on the opposite page. Make sure your answers make sense!

1 The pig lives in a _____ .

2 If you trip over the tree _____ you might _____ yourself.

3 To jump into a burning lake was a very _____ _____ .

4 The _____ was very _____ so it did not break when it hit the sea bed.

5 If you want to enter the Road Safety competition you must _____ your plans for the _____ by tomorrow.

B Read this short passage from a newspaper carefully then use the dictionary page to help you answer the questions that follow it.

Heanley Town Swimming Club starts a new season on Friday 12th August. Membership fees will be £17.50p a year. The ten best swimmers in the club will take part in the National Finals. The three next best swimmers will travel with the team in case someone is injured. All fees must be sent to the treasurer, John Aitken. Jane Sedgeley will drive the minibus.

1 What is the **subject** of this newspaper article?

2 What is the **subscription** to the club?

3 How many **substitutes** will go to the National Finals?

4 To whom do you **submit** your fees?

5 Who is the **subject** of the last sentence?

C If you look at the words printed in red on the dictionary page you will see that they are followed first by words in *italics* telling you what part of speech they are, and then by words in small, bold, black type. These are different versions of the word in red. Fill in the gaps below by using **only** the words that appear on the dictionary page in small, bold, black type.

The _____ from the _____ where the pigs lived filled the air. This smell was so strong it _____ even the _____ of the farm workers. They had to make masks out of very thick _____ before they could get near the pigs. Several of the workers fainted so _____ had to be found.

Skin

This page is from an information book on living things.

THE HUMAN BODY

● The colour of your skin depends on a brown pigment produced in the skin. This pigment, called melanin, is formed by skin cells called melanocytes. Everybody has about the same number of melanocytes but those of dark-skinned people produce more melanin than those of light-skinned people.

When the skin is exposed to strong sunlight more melanin is produced making light skin tan.

When you bleed, platelets send out fibres which trap red cells. Blood then changes into a thick jelly, a blood clot, which blocks the wound.

Some people have areas where melanin concentrates, producing freckles which may increase in number and darken in the sun.

You may notice dark blotches on the back of the hands of old people. They appear because the melanocytes are no longer producing melanin evenly over the whole surface of the skin.

● When you cut yourself the skin is torn and blood leaks out from broken blood vessels. Immediately platelets (bits of bone marrow cells floating in the blood) stick together and collect at the edge of severed blood vessels. These platelets,

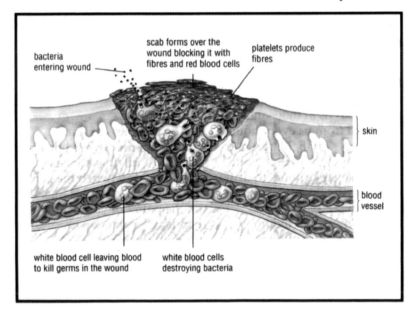

bacteria entering wound

scab forms over the wound blocking it with fibres and red blood cells

platelets produce fibres

skin

blood vessel

white blood cell leaving blood to kill germs in the wound

white blood cells destroying bacteria

A

Under these four questions are several possible answers. Use the opposite page to discover the right answer for each question.

1   What is melanin made from?

| blood vessels | melanocytes | platelets | bone marrow |

2 People with dark skin and people with light skin have about the same number of melanocytes.

| True | False | Can't tell |

3 The melanocytes in a light skinned person produce less melanin than the melanocytes in a dark skinned person.

| True | False | Can't tell |

4 Which one of these makes the skin produce more melanin?

| rainwater | blood vessels | sunlight | fibrin |

B

1 What carries the blood just underneath your skin?

2 When you cut yourself what join up and go to the edge of the cut?

3 What is a scab made out of?

4 What grows underneath a scab?

5 Why is it important to have white blood cells?

C

On the opposite page the information about how the body copes with a cut is passed on to the reader in three ways: short paragraphs of writing

a diagram

captions on the diagram.

Using the same three methods write and draw the following information.

1 How to put on a sock.

2 How to sharpen a pencil.

3 How to make your teacher jump.

Geological time

This chart gives you pictorial information on millions of years of history.

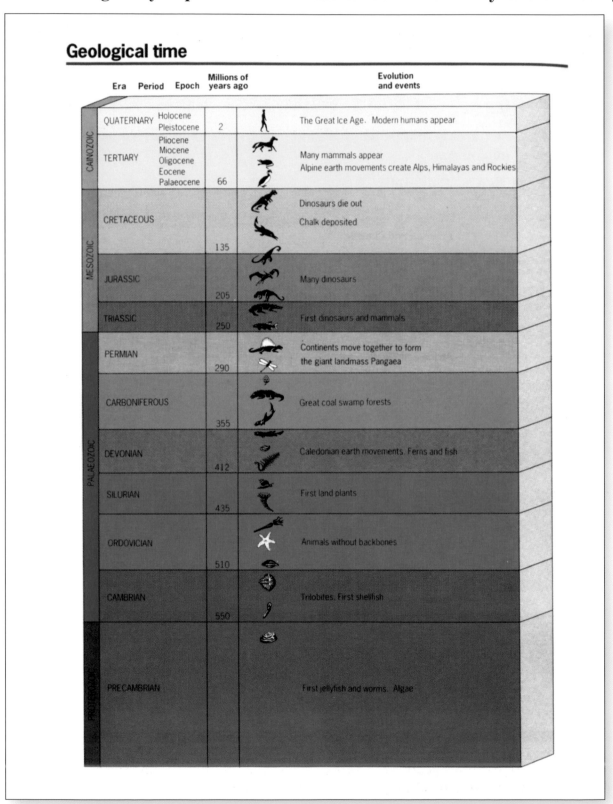

Geological time

Era	Period	Epoch	Millions of years ago		Evolution and events
CAINOZOIC	QUATERNARY	Holocene Pleistocene	2		The Great Ice Age. Modern humans appear
CAINOZOIC	TERTIARY	Pliocene Miocene Oligocene Eocene Palaeocene	66		Many mammals appear Alpine earth movements create Alps, Himalayas and Rockies
MESOZOIC	CRETACEOUS		135		Dinosaurs die out Chalk deposited
MESOZOIC	JURASSIC		205		Many dinosaurs
MESOZOIC	TRIASSIC		250		First dinosaurs and mammals
PALAEOZOIC	PERMIAN		290		Continents move together to form the giant landmass Pangaea
PALAEOZOIC	CARBONIFEROUS		355		Great coal swamp forests
PALAEOZOIC	DEVONIAN		412		Caledonian earth movements. Ferns and fish
PALAEOZOIC	SILURIAN		435		First land plants
PALAEOZOIC	ORDOVICIAN		510		Animals without backbones
PALAEOZOIC	CAMBRIAN		550		Trilobites. First shellfish
PROTEROZOIC	PRECAMBRIAN				First jellyfish and worms. Algae

A

1 How many **eras** appear on the diagram?

2 How many **periods** were there in the Mesozoic era?

3 How many **epochs** were there in the Tertiary period?

4 **a)** Which came first, the **Cretaceous** period or the **Jurassic** period?
b) Why might it be rather frightening to go back to the **Jurassic** period?

5 If you went back to the **Devonian** period, what might you find to eat?

6 How many million years ago did the first **land** plants appear?

B

1 **a)** Did dinosaurs ever live at the same time as human beings?
b) Explain how you can tell this from the chart.

2 **a)** Could a dinosaur have climbed Mount Everest in the Himalayas before the first human being did?
b) Explain how you can tell this from the chart.

3 If someone tried to sell you a fossilized rabbit that they said was 500 million years old, how could the chart tell you they were lying?

4 What was **Pangaea**?

5 The coal people burn on their fires was once a great forest. In which **period** did this forest exist?

6 Name **two** living creatures we still see today that are related to creatures that lived on earth 600 million years ago.

C

The **chart** on the opposite page shows some of the things that happened on Earth over millions of years. Make a similar **chart** showing what happened to you in a school day last week.

Divide your day into different **eras**. The era at the bottom of the chart should be the first part of the day. You might call it the Pre-Breakfast Era.

Divide the eras into **periods**. The At-School Era might include the Lessons Period and the Break Period.

Divide the periods into **epochs**. The Lesson Period might include the Maths Epoch and the Break Period might include the Football Epoch.

Add **events** and how long ago all this took place.

Antarctica

This page is from an A-Z of geography.

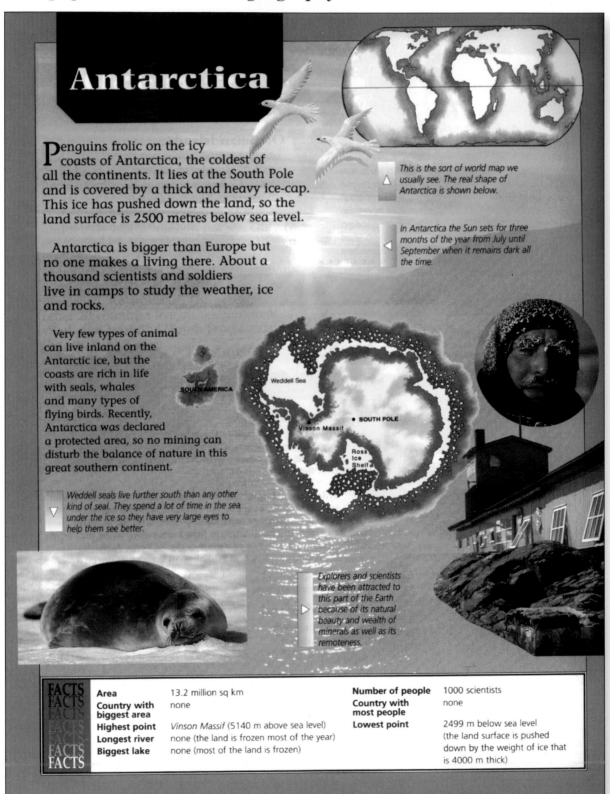

Antarctica

Penguins frolic on the icy coasts of Antarctica, the coldest of all the continents. It lies at the South Pole and is covered by a thick and heavy ice-cap. This ice has pushed down the land, so the land surface is 2500 metres below sea level.

Antarctica is bigger than Europe but no one makes a living there. About a thousand scientists and soldiers live in camps to study the weather, ice and rocks.

Very few types of animal can live inland on the Antarctic ice, but the coasts are rich in life with seals, whales and many types of flying birds. Recently, Antarctica was declared a protected area, so no mining can disturb the balance of nature in this great southern continent.

This is the sort of world map we usually see. The real shape of Antarctica is shown below.

In Antarctica the Sun sets for three months of the year from July until September when it remains dark all the time.

Weddell seals live further south than any other kind of seal. They spend a lot of time in the sea under the ice so they have very large eyes to help them see better.

Explorers and scientists have been attracted to this part of the Earth because of its natural beauty and wealth of minerals as well as its remoteness.

SOUTH AMERICA • Weddell Sea • Vinson Massif • SOUTH POLE • Ross Ice Shelf

FACTS

Area	13.2 million sq km	**Number of people**	1000 scientists
Country with biggest area	none	**Country with most people**	none
Highest point	*Vinson Massif* (5140 m above sea level)	**Lowest point**	2499 m below sea level (the land surface is pushed down by the weight of ice that is 4000 m thick)
Longest river	none (the land is frozen most of the year)		
Biggest lake	none (most of the land is frozen)		

1 Write down the correct answer. Antarctica is:

| a country | a continent | an ice-shelf | an explorer |

2 Name two creatures you might see swimming in the Weddell Sea.

3 What has happened to the land in Antarctica?

4 Why would it be rather boring to visit Antarctica in August?

5 Why is **Vinson Massif** marked on the map of Antarctica?

1 No country owns Antarctica. Why might some countries want to own Antarctica?

2 Why do you think soldiers go to Antarctica?

3 What is the name of the continent that is nearest to Antarctica?

4 Would you **like** or **dislike** to live in Antarctica? Give **two** good reasons to back up your answer.

5 What do you think the birds of Antarctica feed on?

6 Find the word on the opposite page that means **play**.

On the opposite page you are given information about Antarctica in several different ways. There are **maps**. There are **captions** pointing to the photographs. There are **paragraphs** of writing. There is a **factfile** at the bottom of the page.

Using the same four methods of passing information make a page about the room where you are taught, or else a room at home.

Your **factfile** won't contain "longest river" or "biggest lake", but it might have "longest table" and "deepest sink".

Your **map** won't have "Weddell Sea" or "South Pole", but it might have "reading corner" and "wastepaper bin".

Your **paragraphs** won't be about "ice-caps" or "whales", but they might contain information about "radiators" and "your teacher".

How animals send messages

This page is from the *Oxford Children's Book of Science*.

FINDING FOOD

Most animals must find food to survive. Sometimes, they will go to great lengths to avoid sharing it with others. However, some animals will cooperate and communicate in their search for food.

Bees have evolved a very elaborate system of passing on information about the location of food. In a hive, bees perform a dance in which they wiggle their bodies while moving in a particular direction. Using this dance, they can communicate to other bees that there are flowers with a good supply of nectar in a certain direction relative to the Sun. Their movements also give an indication of how far away the supply is.

DANGER AROUND

Many animals have a special call which warns other members of the group when danger is present. This is particularly true of birds, which can produce very loud alarm calls. Near airfields, recordings of bird alarm calls are often played back in order to get rid of flocks that might interfere with the planes. At airfields, humans regard birds as a danger. However, for the birds, the planes are the danger.

Some animals listen for the alarm calls of other creatures to give them warning. Others post sentries to look out for danger and give warnings to the rest of the group. That way, the others can safely concentrate on feeding or drinking. Meerkats are like this. They can stand up almost vertically and swivel their heads through a very wide angle to spot danger approaching.

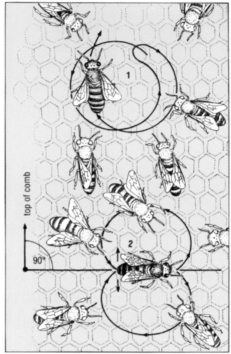
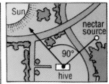

top of comb

90°

Left and above When a worker bee returns to the hive, she does a dance to tell other bees where to find flowers with nectar in. If the flowers are close, she does a simple, round dance (1). But if they are further away, she does a complicated 'waggle' dance (2). The speed at which the tail waggles indicates the distance of the flowers. In the middle part of the dance, her direction relative to the hive gives the direction of the flowers relative to the Sun.

Left Many animals help each other by giving warning of approaching danger. This meerkat in the Kalahari Desert, southern Africa, has been posted as a sentry to stand up as high as possible. His job is to warn the rest of the group if he senses a predator in the area.

A

1 Why do bees dance?

2 If a bee does the simple, round dance, what message is she passing on to the other bees?

3 If a bee does the complicated waggle dance, what message is she passing on to the other bees?

4 What part of her body does a bee use when she is showing how far away the food is?

5 **Two** of these sentences are true. Write them down.
Bees are selfish. Bees cooperate. Bees keep secrets from each other. Bees don't communicate. Bees live alone. Bees use the Sun to find their way.

B

1 How do birds warn each other of danger?

2 Where do meerkats live?

3 What do meerkats do to stop themselves being attacked?

4 Write down the sentence used on the opposite page that tells you **two** different skills the meerkat has that help it spot danger.

5 Explain how humans use the alarm calls of birds to make it safer for humans to fly.

6 Explain how meerkats and bees are similar to each other.

C

On the opposite page there is a great deal of information about the ways bees and meerkats pass messages to each other.

Humans pass messages to each other in many different ways. These include: speech, letters, television, radio, books, magazines, newspapers, postcards and computers.

Imagine you wake up one morning and find you have turned into a bee. You still think like a human but you can't speak and your legs can't hold a pen or pencil. How will you pass a message to your friends telling them what has happened to you? How will you pass your message without frightening them? Write an account suggesting how you manage to pass the message.

What clothes are made of

This page is from an information book.

What clothes are made of

There are many different kinds of clothes, for many different purposes. Some clothes are worn for warmth; and when the weather is hot, we like to wear clothes that are cool. People who do hard work outside need clothes that are tough and do not easily wear out. When we dress up to go to a party we wear 'party' clothes, and for playing games we often wear special clothes. Some clothes are brightly coloured and some are plain. Dyes are used to colour materials for clothing.

Cloth can be made from many different materials and some of them are described on these two pages.

Wool

1 The material we know as wool, comes from sheep.

2 Wool is especially good for clothes that are warm to wear.

Cotton

3 Cotton comes from a bush, about 1 metre tall, that needs about six months of hot, moist weather to flower and produce seeds. When the seed cases ripen, they split open. The seeds inside are in a ball of fluffy-white cotton. Cotton can be picked by machine, but most of it is still picked by hand.

4 Cotton is good for making clothes that are cool. Summer dresses and shirts are often made from cotton cloth.

Silk

5 Silkworms are really caterpillars. They live on mulberry leaves which are their only food. Like all other caterpillars, silkworms make cocoons to live in while they change into moths and it is the threads they use to make their cocoons that are unwound and made into silk.

6 Silkworms make their threads by squirting liquids from their bodies. When the liquids meet the air, they set into silk threads.

7 Silk is an expensive material and is often used to make clothes for special occasions. Some men's ties are made of silk.

A

1 What do silkworms eat?

2 What do silkworms turn into?

3 What do silkworms make out of silk?

4 Why do you think silk is more expensive than wool?

B

1 You are making a wedding dress for your sister. The wedding is a very special occasion. Which material do you choose?

2 After your sister is married she is going to live on a farm on a cold island near Iceland. She will need warm clothes. What animals should she keep?

3 If you had a job picking cotton would you wear clothes made from:

silk, cotton or **wool**?

When you have made your choice explain why you decided this was the best material for this particular job.

4 What is the word used on the opposite page that means the substances that colour cloth?

C

Here are fact files on three countries.

	Gregoria	Kanzania	Lothlorizstan
Rainfall	Heavy	Light	Average
Temperature	Cold	Average	Hot
Typical countryside	Grassland	Woodland	Open fields

1 a) Which **one** of these countries would be best for producing silk?
b) Give **one** reason why you chose this country.

2 a) In which country could the people grow cotton **and** wear clothes made from cotton?
b) Give **two** reasons to explain why you chose this country.

3 a) You have not yet chosen **one** of the three countries. What material do you think the people in this country should make their clothes from?
b) Do you think this country is suited to producing this material? Give **two** reasons to explain why you think it will, or will not, be able to produce this material.

Space technology

This page is from an A-Z of technology.

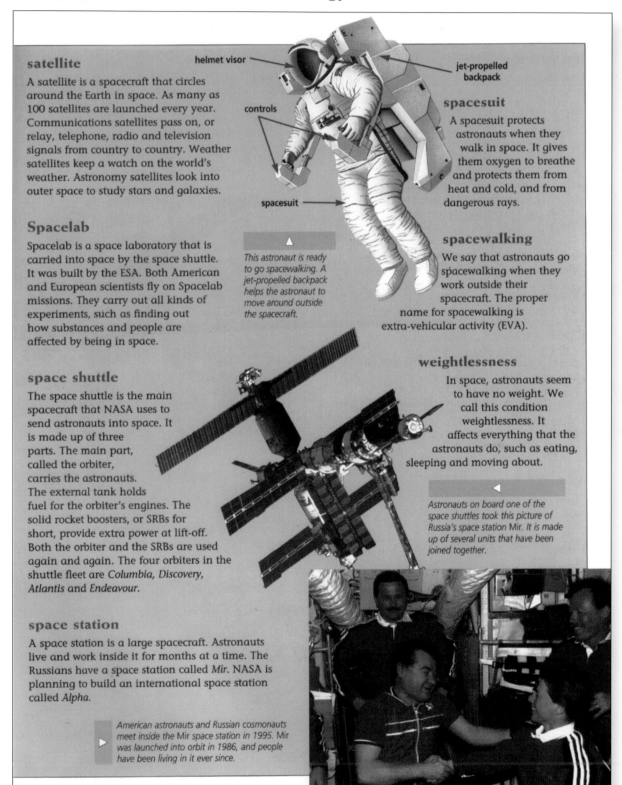

satellite

A satellite is a spacecraft that circles around the Earth in space. As many as 100 satellites are launched every year. Communications satellites pass on, or relay, telephone, radio and television signals from country to country. Weather satellites keep a watch on the world's weather. Astronomy satellites look into outer space to study stars and galaxies.

Spacelab

Spacelab is a space laboratory that is carried into space by the space shuttle. It was built by the ESA. Both American and European scientists fly on Spacelab missions. They carry out all kinds of experiments, such as finding out how substances and people are affected by being in space.

space shuttle

The space shuttle is the main spacecraft that NASA uses to send astronauts into space. It is made up of three parts. The main part, called the orbiter, carries the astronauts. The external tank holds fuel for the orbiter's engines. The solid rocket boosters, or SRBs for short, provide extra power at lift-off. Both the orbiter and the SRBs are used again and again. The four orbiters in the shuttle fleet are *Columbia*, *Discovery*, *Atlantis* and *Endeavour*.

space station

A space station is a large spacecraft. Astronauts live and work inside it for months at a time. The Russians have a space station called *Mir*. NASA is planning to build an international space station called *Alpha*.

helmet visor

controls

spacesuit

jet-propelled backpack

This astronaut is ready to go spacewalking. A jet-propelled backpack helps the astronaut to move around outside the spacecraft.

spacesuit

A spacesuit protects astronauts when they walk in space. It gives them oxygen to breathe and protects them from heat and cold, and from dangerous rays.

spacewalking

We say that astronauts go spacewalking when they work outside their spacecraft. The proper name for spacewalking is extra-vehicular activity (EVA).

weightlessness

In space, astronauts seem to have no weight. We call this condition weightlessness. It affects everything that the astronauts do, such as eating, sleeping and moving about.

Astronauts on board one of the space shuttles took this picture of Russia's space station Mir. It is made up of several units that have been joined together.

American astronauts and Russian cosmonauts meet inside the Mir space station in 1995. Mir was launched into orbit in 1986, and people have been living in it ever since.

1 List **three** types of signals that are passed on by satellites.

2 Do astronomy satellites or weather satellites look towards Earth?

3 What is **Mir**?

4 a) What do the initials **SRB** stand for?
   b) What do **SRB**s help carry into space?

5 a) What do the intials **EVA** stand for?
   b) What would you have to wear if you went on an **EVA**?

6 What are **Columbia**, **Endeavour**, and **Discovery**?

1 a) What do Americans call people who go into space?
   b) What do Russians call people who go into space?

2 What evidence is there on the opposite page that the Americans and the Russians work together in space?

3 a) What is the biggest change that comes over the human body in space?
   b) How do you think this affects the way space travellers move?

4 Name **two** jobs a spacesuit is designed to do.

You have been asked to help write a new dictionary. This is how the dictionary is set out:

satellite   Spacecraft that circles around the Earth in space. Used for relaying electronic signals, checking on the weather, studying outer space.

You are not allowed to use more than 20 words for each entry.
Use the information on the opposite page to write the entries for these words

backpack
orbiter
relay
visor

Impressionism

This page is from a book called *What is Art?*

Claude Monet, 'The Beach at Trouville', 1870, oil on canvas, 38 x 46 cm.

This oil painting by Claude Monet (1840–1926), *The Beach at Trouville*, really was painted on the beach. He was spending a holiday in Trouville with his wife Camille (on the left) and their small son, Jean. The woman in the black dress may be Madame Boudin, the wife of Eugène Boudin, a painter friend. Perhaps the little red beach shoe on the chair belongs to Jean.

This photograph (much magnified) of a detail of the painting shows sand from the beach stuck in the paint, blown there by the wind.

Working in the open air

Ever since artists had taken to painting pictures of landscapes, in the 18th century, they had made sketches on the spot, out of doors. But it didn't occur to them to paint the final picture itself out of doors. What you did out of doors was the raw material for your painting. 'Proper' painting was something you did in your studio, with all your paints and equipment at hand.

But when the Impressionist painters began to experiment with colour and ways to show light, they found they wanted to work out of doors. It wasn't just a question of the light. They felt that somehow work done out of doors was more 'honest' and 'true'. They could observe nature closely, and catch the quickly changing effects of the weather.

It became the fashion to work that way, and to use lightweight equipment that could be folded up and easily carried around. The new paints, based on chemicals instead of natural pigments, were in tubes, and convenient to pack. But many of the Impressionists took their paintings back to their studios to finish them off. Monet said he never had a proper studio. He used a boat. Later, when he lived in the country at Giverny, he had a room that served both as studio and sitting room.

To us it no longer seems unusual to work out of doors. In fact some modern artists have worked under very extreme weather conditions. The Scottish artist, Joan Eardley (1921–1963), who lived on the very windy east coast of Scotland, used to weight her canvas down with stones, so that it wouldn't blow away!

This painting by Edouard Manet (1832–1883) shows Monet in his boat, set up as an outdoor studio.

Edouard Manet, 'Monet Working in his Boat', 1874, 80x 98 cm.

A

1 What is the name given to a quick drawing made on the spot?

2 What was the room called where an 18th century artist would finish painting a picture?

3 a) How did the painter Monet work differently to the 18th century painters?
b) Name an unusual place where Monet used to finish his pictures.

4 Why did the Impressionist painters like the new chemical paints?

5 Where did Monet go on his holidays?

B

1 a) What is the best piece of evidence on the opposite page that proves Monet painted out of doors? (It **isn't** written evidence!)
b) What other piece of evidence appears on the same page that suggests Monet painted out of doors? (It **isn't** written evidence!)

2 What evidence is there in the caption to the picture at the top of the page that suggests Monet went on holidays with other artists?

3 What evidence is there on the opposite page that suggests Monet's artist friends came and worked with him?

4 Use the evidence on the opposite page to show that people in 1870 spent their time at the seaside very differently compared to nowadays.

5 What did Joan Eardley have in common with Monet?

C

If you can prove something by using **evidence** you have proved something is **true**, it is a **fact**.

If you think something, but have no **evidence** to prove it, then it is your **opinion**. Read the passage below carefully. When you have finished make a list of four **facts** that appear in it and a list of four **opinions** that appear in it.

It had rained so hard the river had flooded. The ducks thought it was the best weather ever. The people who were caught without their umbrellas said it was dreadful. Then the lightning hit the huge oak tree and a huge branch fell off. It floated towards the ruined bridge. Sam, who climbed on and drifted to dry land, thought it made a marvellous boat. Jamal, who was knocked out when it hit him on the head as he swam home, wasn't so sure.

A Small Dragon

This poem is a mixture of the ordinary and the extraordinary.

A Small Dragon

I've found a small dragon in the woodshed.
Think it must have come from deep inside a forest
because it's damp and green and leaves
are still reflecting in its eyes.

I fed it on many things, tried grass,
the roots of stars, hazel-nut and dandelion,
but it stared up at me as if to say, I need
foods you can't provide.

It made a nest among the coal,
not unlike a bird's but larger,
it is out of place here
and is quite silent.

If you believed in it I would come
hurrying to your house to let you share my wonder,
but I want instead to see
if you yourself will pass this way.

Brian Patten

1 a) What did the poet keep in his woodshed?
b) What did the poet find in his woodshed?

2 The poet thinks the dragon came from a wood. Write down **one** reason the poet gives to explain why he thinks it comes from a wood.

3 a) List **two** common animal foods the poet tried to feed to the dragon.
b) Write down the most extraordinary food the poet offered to the dragon.

4 a) What did the dragon make in the woodshed?
b) What did the dragon use as its building materials?

5 Write down the line in the poem that tells you about the sort of noises the dragon made.

1 Why do you think the poet says the dragon is **out of place** in the shed?

2 a) In the first verse the poet says the leaves from the forest are still reflecting in the dragon's eyes. Do you think this is **possible**, or **impossible**?
b) If you think it is **possible** explain how the forest leaves are reflecting in the dragon's eyes even though the dragon isn't in the forest.

If you think it is **impossible** explain what you think the poet is trying to tell us about the dragon's eyes when he says they reflect the leaves.

3 What do you have to do before the poet will come to your house?

Try writing a poem about a very extraordinary discovery in a very ordinary place.

Four Children, One Being.
Four Children, One Seeing.

The small ship
Came down in the garden
Hardly disturbing the night.
The Being stepped out
As it landed,
Walking upright.
Its fur was like frost
In the moonshine
Sparkling with light.
It was as tall as I
No more—
It looked into my eyes
And knew me sure as sure.
I wanted to show that I liked it,
I wanted to smile—
I tried—
But it set no store
By anything I knew—
I cried...

No No!
The ship was huge —
The Alien too
But it had no form —
Like fog it was
You could see right through
Eyes it had, I think,
That floated round inside it
Like diamonds they were,
Faceted and prism'd
That surely denied it
Any sight as we see,
The coldness of it
Was space grown
It wasn't anything that could be known
Or could know me
It turned the colour of things to grey.
I was terrified —
I ran away!

Not at all!
The ship was small
But did not touch the ground.
The thing rolled out sounding laughter
And bounced around.
It shot out a sort of hand
And showed me in the palm
Stars and planets wheeling.
I thought it meant no harm
Though it whirled around and round me,
Dizzied me and sent me reeling—
I thought it was playing.
It showed me toys and treasure and keys,
Come — come with these, it said,
In no voice that I heard
But I saw that it shrank
From touching trees
And I said, without word—
I'm staying.

I was watching from the window.
What made you act so weird?
Why did you cry
And run
As though you saw something
you feared?

Were you playing a game?
Or did something give you a
scare?

I watched from the window
All the time —
And I saw nothing there!

Julie Holder

Four Children, One Being

Four children are in the same place at the same time. Each child uses a different coloured piece of paper to write down what they see. In the questions the children are called by these colours.

1 Where did Green say the alien space ship landed?

2 Where was Blue when the space ship landed?

3 What did Green say the alien's skin was like?

4 What did Orange say was unusual about the alien's body?

5 Who said that the alien had a hand?

6 What did Green want to tell the alien?

7 What did Orange do after seeing the alien?

1 What reason does Yellow give to explain why she didn't go away with the alien?

2 Why did Yellow become dizzy?

3 **a)** How do you think Yellow and the alien "spoke" to each other?
   b) Write down a line from Yellow's sheet of paper that shows that they **didn't** speak using human voices.

4 How was Blue's experience different to the experience of the other three children?

5 Which one of the other children do you think Blue was talking to when she asked: "Were you playing a game?"

6 **a)** Which of the children seems to have seen something that at least slightly resembled a human?
   b) Write down **one** line from this child's description of the alien that makes you think that what this child saw looked quite like a human.

7 **a)** Which one of the four children would **you** like to be?
   b) Give a good reason to explain why you would choose to have the same experience as this person.

The four children seem to have seen four very different things. Blue didn't see anything the others saw. Green and Yellow agree that the space ship was small, but otherwise Green, Yellow and Orange seem to disagree about almost everything else!

Perhaps the alien appeared differently to each of them.
Perhaps it was like a mirror.
Perhaps it reflected the different ways the different children thought.

If this is true:

1 Which one of the children had no imagination?

2 Which one of the children was expecting something terrible?

3 Which one of the children was looking for fun?

4 Which one of the children was looking for a friend?

Imagine you are **one** of these children, Green, Orange, Yellow or Blue.
Imagine the alien comes again.

This time you go inside the alien space ship.

Remember, everything in the spaceship will reflect the way you are thinking!
If you are expecting it to be terrifying, it will be.
If you are expecting it to be fun, it will be.
If you are expecting it to be the home of someone you would like to be friends with, it will be!

Write down an account of your experience.

You can write your account in different ways:

1 You can write it as a **story**.

2 You can write it in the form of a **letter** you drop from the space ship just before it zooms off into outer space.

3 You can write it like the four other children did, as a **poem**.

Some of the lines in their poems are long, some are short. Some lines rhyme with other lines, some don't. In their poems the children have used strong pieces of description: "Its fur was like frost", "Like diamonds they were", "Stars and plants wheeling".

In your poem you can choose how long or how short you will make the lines and whether they will rhyme or not. But make sure you use strong pieces of description.

Posting Letters

There are no lamps in our village,
And when the owl-and-bat black night
Creeps up low fields
And sidles along the manor walls
I walk quickly.

It is winter;
The letters patter from my hand
Into the tin box in the cottage wall;
The gate taps behind me,
And the road in the silver of moonlight
Gleams greasily
Where the tractors have stood.

I have to go under the spread fingers of the trees
Under the dark windows of the old man's house,
Where the panes in peeling frames
Flash like spectacles
As I tip-toe.
But there is no sound of him in his one room
In the Queen-Anne shell,
Behind the shutters.

I run past the gates,
Their iron feet gaitered with grass,
Into the church porch,
Standing, hand on the cold door ring,
While above
The tongue-tip of the clock
Clops
Against the hard palate of the tower.
The door groans as I push
And
Dare myself to dash
Along the flagstones to the great brass bird,
To put one shrinking hand
Upon the gritty lid.
Of Black Tom's tomb.

Don't tempt whatever spirits stir
In this damp corner,
But
Race down the aisle,
Blunder past font,
Fumble the door,
Leap steps,
Clang iron gate,
And patter through the short-cut muddy lane.

Oh, what a pumping of breath
And choking throat
For three letters.
And now there are the cattle
Stirring in the straw
So close

I can hear their soft muzzling and coughs;
And there are the bungalows,
And the steel-blue miming of the little screen;
And the familiar rattle of the latch,
And our own knocker
Clicking like an old friend;
And
I am home.

Gregory Harrison

Posting Letters

The answers to Section A can be found in the first three verses.

1 Why has the poet, the person telling this story, gone out in the dark?

2 Why is it so dark in this particular village?

3 **a)** Where does the light that shines on the road come from?
   b) What is it on the road that gleams in this light?

4 Who lives in the first frightening building the poet has to pass?

5 **a)** The poet says the trees have **spread fingers**. What do you think the poet is talking about when he says the trees have fingers?
   b) What do you think the poet wants you to feel the trees may do with their **fingers**?

6 What does the poet say are like **spectacles**?

7 Write down the **line** from the third verse of the poem that shows the poet went past the house as quietly as possible.

8 Why can't the poet see through some of the windows?

9 The words **Queen Anne shell** mean that the house was built almost three hundred years ago in the time of Queen Anne and that much of the house was empty, like a shell you might find on a beach.
   Write down another line from the third verse that shows much of the house was empty.

10 Write down a **word** from the first verse of the poem that shows the darkness comes upon the poet without him noticing it.

11 Write down **two** words used in the second verse of the poem that describe two different sounds the poet hears.

12 Sometimes the poet uses many words in a line:
   "I have to go under the spread fingers of the trees"
   Sometimes the poet uses only a few words in a line:
   "It is winter;"

   a) Write down a short line in which the words all start with the same letter.
   b) Write down **two** short lines that describe how the poet moves.

The answers to Section B can be found in verses 4, 5, 6 and 7.

1 Which building does the poet enter after he has passed the iron gates?

2 Write down the word that the poet uses to describe the sound of the clock.

3 What part of the clock do you think is the **tongue-tip**?

4 a) The poet makes the church door seem alive, like a human. Write down the word the poet uses to make the door seem as though it is alive.
   b) How do you think the poet wants us to feel when we hear this word?

5 The poet has gone into the church for a dare. What does the poet dare himself to touch?

6 The poet describes his hand as **shrinking**. His hand isn't really getting smaller, so what do you think the poet means when he says his hand is "**shrinking** upon the gritty lid"?

7 In the fifth verse the poet wants to show us how frightened he is when he runs out of the church. To do this he leaves out some of the words so the story races past us just like the poet races through the church.
   Add words to this line so that it makes a complete sentence:

   "Clang iron gate"

8 Why does the poet choose to go down the muddy lane?

9 What does the poet mean when he uses the words:

   "a pumping of breath"?

10 What are the first friendly things the poet comes across?

11 What is the poet talking about when he mentions the:

   "steel-blue miming of the little screen"?

12 Write down the **two** things that give out comforting sounds when the poet arrives home.

The poet uses a mixture of long lines and short lines. He makes many of the things in the poem act or sound and look like humans – the darkness **creeps**, the trees have **spread fingers**, the gates have **iron feet**. The poet uses strong descriptive words – **blunder, fumble, leap, dash**.

Using the same ideas write a poem of your own about:

"The Haunted House"

The Pardoner's Tale

Chaucer

Life went on during the war. People carried on with their daily tasks, soldiers left for France, merchants bought and sold things and bands of pilgrims trooped off to the shrines of saints. Geoffrey Chaucer, the greatest of the early English poets, who had worked for Henry V's father, tells of such a group travelling to Canterbury.

His pilgrims are of all sorts, good people and bad. One of the least attractive is the Pardoner. He pretends he can forgive people's sins and stop them going to Hell when they die. He will pardon anyone who can pay him.

The pilgrims take it in turns to tell the others a story. Thus the journey to Canterbury will seem shorter. The Pardoner sees his chance to make some money. This is the story he entertains his fellow pilgrims with.

WITHOUT STOPPING TO THANK HIM, THE THREE SCAMPER OFF TO THE OAK TREE. THE YOUTH GETS THERE FIRST. HE GASPS AND POINTS...

AS SOON AS HE HAS GONE, THE TWO MEN PLOT TO KILL THE YOUTH WHEN HE COMES BACK. THEN THERE WILL BE MORE MONEY FOR EACH OF THEM.

WHEN THE YOUTH RETURNS THEY DRAW THEIR DAGGERS AND STAB HIM TO DEATH. THE MEN LAUGH AND DRINK THE WINE.

LITTLE DO THEY KNOW THAT THE YOUTH HAS BEEN PLOTTING TOO, AND HAS POISONED THE WINE!

TWO MEN AND A YOUTH ARE DRINKING IN A TAVERN. A COFFIN PASSES BY. SOMEONE ASKS WHO THE DEAD MAN WAS. 'A FRIEND OF YOURS,' HE IS TOLD. 'LAST NIGHT, WHILE HE WAS DRUNK, A THIEF CALLED DEATH STOLE HIS LIFE AWAY. HE'S STOLEN MANY LIVES IN THESE PARTS.' ONE OF THE MEN SUGGESTS 'WE OUGHT TO HUNT DOWN THIS THIEF CALLED DEATH!'

THE THREE AGREE TO GO AND LOOK FOR DEATH. THEY MEET AN OLD MAN WHO TELLS THEM THAT HE KNOWS DEATH WELL. 'I'M SO OLD AND FEEBLE THAT I'M READY FOR DEATH BUT HE WON'T HAVE ME. IF YOU WANT TO MEET HIM GO TO THAT OAK TREE UP THE LANE. THAT'S WHERE I LAST SAW HIM.'

THE OTHER TWO SEE WHAT HAS STARTLED HIM. THERE IS A GREAT HEAP OF GOLD SPILLING OUT FROM THE HOLLOW TREE. THEY FORGET ABOUT DEATH AND GET VERY EXCITED OVER WHAT THEY WILL DO WITH THE MONEY.

'WE MUSN'T BE SEEN TAKING IT AWAY IN DAYLIGHT! WE'LL HAVE TO WAIT UNTIL IT'S DARK.' THE MEN SEND THE YOUTH BACK TO THE TAVERN FOR DRINK.

THE MEN CLUTCH THEIR THROATS AND COLLAPSE ON TO THE GRASS. NOW THERE ARE THREE CORPSES BY THE TREE.

THEIR WISH HAS BEEN GRANTED; THEY HAVE FOUND DEATH!

The Pardoner ends his story and tells the pilgrims that the drinkers were punished for their greed.

'If you good people want to escape Hell,' he says, 'I can let you have a pardon for the sin of greed. It won't cost you much!'

When the pilgrims realize that his story was not meant to amuse but to make money, they are angry at the way they have been tricked. They will not give him anything and it is quite a while before they will even speak to him again.

The Pardoner's Tale

The questions in Section A are about the man who tells the story.

1 A shrine is a holy place that people visit. Which one of these words is the proper name for people who go on a journey to visit these holy shrines?
merchants   soldiers   poets   pilgrims   saints

2 What was the name of the man who wrote stories about these travellers?

3 What did a Pardoner do in return for your money?

4 Where are the Pardoner and the other travellers going?

5 What do the Pardoner and the other travellers do to pass the time?

6 Why does the Pardoner tell this particular story?

7 Why are the other travellers angry with the Pardoner?

8 What **two** things do the other travellers do because they are so angry?

The questions in Section B are about the story he tells.

1 How many people are drinking together in the tavern?

2 What attracts their attention?

3 How can you tell from what they say that the people in the tavern have drunk too much?

4 Where does the old man tell them they will find Death?

5 How are the friends rude to the old man?

6 Why do you think the youth gets there first?

7 What does the youth do that tells you he is surprised?

8 Why was the youth surprised?

9 What do the friends stop thinking about when they reach the hollow tree?

10 Why do you think the men say they must wait until it is dark?

11 Why is the youth sent back to the tavern?

12 Why do the men decide they will kill the youth?

13 What do the men do **after** the murder that shows you they have never been real friends with the youth.

14 Explain how the youth gets his revenge even though he is dead.

15 a) Do you think it was fair that the two men died?
  b) Give a good reason to back up your answer.

16 a) Do you think it was fair that the youth died?
  b) Give a good reason to back up your answer.

17 Write down the word that you think caused the death of all three of these people.

kindness   revenge   greed   stupidity   cunning

18 Find the word in the story that means **dead bodies**.

19 Find the word in the story that means **surprised**.

20 What do you think this story teaches you?

The Pardoner's Tale was written by Geoffrey Chaucer as a poem. Because it was written over 600 years ago some of the spellings look rather strange to us. In some places Chaucer has used words that no longer exist! This is the two men speaking after they have killed the youth.

"Now lat us sitte and drynke, and make us merie,
And afterwards we wol his body berie."

1 Turn the lines above into modern English, use a dictionary to help you with any spellings you are not sure of.

2 Where in the story do you think these lines come?

And everich of thise riotures ran
Til he cam to that tree, and ther they founde
Of floryns fyne of gold ycoyned rounde

3 Turn the lines above into modern English. A **florin** was a coin about the size of a ten pence piece. **Everich, riotures** and **ycoyned** are words that are no longer used, but they are very similar to modern words that mean the same thing! See if you can work out what it all means!

Bro Tiger Goes Dead

by James Berry

Tiger swears he's going to crack up Anancy's bones once and for all.

Tiger goes to bed. Bro Tiger lies down in his bed, all still and stiff, wrapped up in a sheet. Bro Tiger says to himself, 'I know that Anancy will come and look at me. The brute will want to make sure I'm dead. He'll want to see how I look when I'm dead. That's when I'm going to collar him up. Oh, how I'm going to grab that Anancy and finish him!'

Bro Tiger calls his wife. He tells his wife she should begin to bawl. She should bawl and cry and wail as loud as she can. She should stand in the yard, put her hands on the top of her head and holler to let everybody know her husband is dead. And Mrs Tiger does that.

Mrs Tiger bawls and bawls so loud that people begin to wonder if all her family is dead suddenly and not just her husband.

Village people come and crowd in the yard, quick-quick. Everybody is worried and sad and full of sympathy. The people talk to one another saying, 'Fancy how Bro Tiger is dead, sudden-sudden.'

'Yes! Fancy how he's dead sudden-sudden. All dead and gone!'

Anancy also hears the mournful death howling. When Anancy hears it, listen to the Anancy to himself. 'Funny how Bro Tiger is dead. Bro Tiger is such a strong and healthy man. Bro Tiger is such a well-fed man. Bro Tiger is dead and I've heard nothing about his sickness.'

Anancy finds himself at Tiger's yard, like the rest of the crowd.

Straightaway, Anancy says to his son, 'Tacooma, did you happen to hear Bro Tiger had an illness?'

Tacooma shakes his head. 'No, no. Heard nothing at all.'

Anancy goes to Dog. 'Bro Dog, did you happen to hear Bro Tiger had an illness?'

Bro Dog shakes his head. 'No, no. Heard nothing at all.'

Anancy goes to Monkey and Puss and Ram-Goat and Jackass and Patoo and asks the same question. Everyone gives a sad shake of the head and says, 'No, no. Heard nothing at all.'

The crowd surrounds Anancy. Everybody starts up saying, 'Bro Tiger showed no sign of illness. Death happened so sudden-sudden, Bro Nancy. So sudden-sudden!'

Anancy says, 'Did anybody call a doctor?'

The people shake their heads and say, 'That would have been no use, Bro Nancy. No use at all.'

'Before death came on, did Tiger call the name of the Lord? Did he whimper? Did he cry out?'

'He didn't have time, Bro Nancy. He didn't have the time,' everybody says. 'It was all so sudden.'

Listen to Anancy now, talking at the top of his voice.

'What kind of man is Tiger? Doesn't Tiger know that no good man can meet his Blessed Lord sudden-sudden and not shudder and cry out?'

Tiger hears Anancy. Tiger feels stupid. Tiger feels he has made a silly mistake. Bro Tiger gives the loudest roar he has ever made.

Anancy bursts out laughing. Anancy says, 'Friends, did you hear that? Did you hear that? Has anyone ever heard a dead man cry out?'

Nobody answers Anancy. Everybody sees that he is right.

By the time Bro Tiger jumps out of the sheet on the bed to come after Anancy, the Anancy is gone. Bro Nancy is well away.

Nobody even talks to Bro Tiger now. Everybody just leaves Bro Tiger's place without a single word.

Bro Tiger Goes Dead

The questions in Section A are all about what happens in the story.

1 Who is Tiger planning to trap?

2 What is Tiger planning to do to his victim if he does trap him?

3 What is Tiger pretending to be when he lies down "still and stiff"?

4 Why does Tiger think this will make his great enemy come and see him?

5 Why does Tiger get his wife to make so much noise?

6 Why does Tiger's wife go outside to bawl and holler?

7 Tiger's wife makes a great deal of noise. What do people think when they hear her making so much noise?

8 In what sort of place do Tiger and his wife live?

9 Why are the local people surprised to hear Mrs Tiger's news?

10 How do the local people feel when they hear Mrs Tiger's sad news?

11 Anancy gives several reasons why he thinks it is strange that Tiger is dead. Write down **two** of the things Anancy says that show Anancy is surprised to hear that Tiger is dead.

12 What does Anancy do that Tiger had wanted him to do?

13 What relation is Anancy to Tacooma?

14 When Anancy is outside Tiger's house he begins to grow suspicious. How can you tell that Anancy is suspicious?

15 Why do the others tell Anancy there was no point calling a doctor?

16 Why does Anancy suddenly start talking loudly, at the top of his voice?

17 Explain clearly why Tiger felt he had to roar.

18 What did everyone realise when Tiger roared?

The questions in Section B are about the way the writer wrote the story and about the different characters who appear in the story.

1 You can tell Tiger really hates Anancy by the words he uses. Choose **one** word from the first sentence that shows you Tiger really wants to hurt Anancy.

2 When Tiger is in bed he uses another word that shows he thinks Anancy is horrible. What does he call Anancy?

3 Which word does Tiger use that shows he means to grab Anancy around the neck?

4 The writer uses several words to make us realise just how much noise Mrs Tiger makes. List **four** different words that describe the noises Mrs Tiger makes.

5 What does Anancy do that shows he is very clever?

6 What does Tiger do that shows he is very stupid?

7 What does Tiger try and do once his trick is discovered?

8 **a)** When the trick is discovered how do the people feel about Tiger?
 b) Why do you think they feel like this about Tiger?

9 What is the other name Anancy is called during the story?

10 How would you write "sudden-sudden" in everyday English?

This story is mainly told through **speech**. The writer tells us what Tiger says to himself and to his wife. We hear what the people say to each other in the yard. Most important of all we hear what Anancy says to the others and how his questions and their answers lead to the discovery of Tiger's trick.

Imagine Tiger tries another trick. First of all he makes a very strong sleeping potion. Then he invites everyone to a fancy dress party. The whole village, Bro Dog, Ram-Goat, Jackass, Monkey, Tacooma, Puss, everyone comes to the party. When his house is full of guests all laughing and singing he tells Mrs Tiger to put the sleeping potion in all the glasses except his. Tiger says that when everyone is asleep he will be able to look under their masks and discover which one is Anancy. Then he will eat him! When Mrs Tiger brings him the tray of glasses Tiger hands them around. Within a few minutes everyone is wide awake, except Tiger! Anancy's fancy dress is a costume that makes him look exactly like Mrs Tiger!

Tell this story by using **speech**.

Like Dog, Like Dad

W. K. McNeil

A man was prowling around his house and he got hungry. His wife was off somewhere—might have been a club meeting; she'd gone somewhere. He was hungry; looking around for something to eat and happened to find a biscuit lying on the radiator. Some kind of biscuit! He didn't know what kind it was; it was just a biscuit. He was hungry. He tried it and he liked it. He ate it and then after his wife got home he said to her, 'What kind of biscuit was that on the radiator?'

'Why do you ask?' she replied. 'What it was was one of the dog biscuits.'

'Well now, I was hungry and I didn't know what kind of biscuit it was and I thought I'd try it and I did and it was good.'

'It was a dog biscuit and you shouldn't have eaten it.'

'Well, I was hungry and I didn't know what kind of biscuit it was and I thought I'd try it and I did and it was good.'

'Oh now, you'd better not do that,' she replied.

'Now, I want some more of them and when you do your shopping get some more dog biscuits.'

'Well, then, if that is what you want.'

So the next time she went marketing she bought just twice as many dog biscuits as she was in the habit of buying. And the clerk who had watched her in her buying for quite a while noted she was buying twice as many dog biscuits. She'd always bought the same amount every time.

'Buying twice as many?' the employee said. 'I see you're buying twice as many dog biscuits. Have you got another dog?'

'No, I don't have another dog. It's just that my husband happened to get hold of a dog biscuit the other day and he didn't know what it was. He ate it and he was hungry and he ate it. I wasn't at home. He ate it; he was hungry so he ate it. And when I came home he asked me what kind it was and I told him. He said he wanted some more of them, so that is why I'm buying twice as many.'

'Now,' the clerk said, 'you better not encourage him to eat those dog biscuits, they might make him sick. They might not be good for him.' But she went ahead and got them anyway.

She went ahead getting them regularly for quite a little spell. Then finally, she went in to do her shopping and just got her old original number that she'd got when she was just feeding the dog. The clerk again observed the different size order. 'You're only getting the amount you used to get when you were only buying for your dog? What is the matter? Is your husband getting tired of dog biscuits and not wanting any more?'

'Oh, it's not that! My husband is dead. My husband is dead.'

'I'm sorry to hear that, but I warned you. I told you they might make him sick. They might hurt him.'

'Oh, no, no they didn't. He got killed!'

'Got killed? How?'

'Chasing cars,' she replied.

Like Dog, Like Dad

The questions in Section A are all about what happens in the story and what you learn about the different characters in the story.

1 How can you tell from the story that the man knows hardly anything about food?

2 What does the woman tell the man he shouldn't have done?

3 **a)** What does the man tell the woman he wants her to do when she goes shopping?
   b) What does the woman say to this?
   c) What does this tell you about the man?

4 What was the first thing that surprised the clerk in the shop?

5 What did the clerk think was the reason the woman had changed the amount she bought?

6 What does the clerk think might happen to the man?

7 **a)** Does the woman take any notice of the clerk?
   b) What does this tell you about the woman?

8 What is the next thing the clerk notices?

9 Why does the clerk think the woman has changed again?

10 What does the woman tell the clerk has happened?

11 Why does the clerk think this has happened?

12 What does the woman tell the clerk has happened?

13 Why do you think the man was doing this when he was killed?

14 Do you think the woman is upset by the news? Give a good reason to back up your answer.

15 Do you feel sorry for the man? Give a good reason to back up your answer.

The questions in Section B are all about the way in which the writer tells the story.

1 Write down the word the writer uses in the first paragraph that makes the man seem to be acting like a dog **before** he eats the biscuit.

2 Find a word the writer uses that means the same as **shopping**.

3 The writer makes the man find the biscuit he eats on a radiator. Why do you think he didn't make him find it on a table or in a tin? What is the writer trying to tell us about the man?

4 If you were reading this story out loud what sort of voice would you give the man? Explain why you would make him sound like this.

5 **a)** If you were reading this story out loud what sort of voice would you give the woman at the **start** of the story? Explain why you would make her sound like this.

b) If you were reading this story out loud what sort of voice would you give the woman at the **end** of the story? Explain why you would make her sound like this.

This story has a **punchline**. A **punchline** is when the writer saves the joke to the very end, to the very last sentence.

When most people read the story you have just read for the first time they expect to find that the man has been poisoned by the dog biscuits. It's a surprise to find he's become just like the animal whose food he's eating.

Here is the end of another story with its **punchline**.
Write the rest of the story that goes before it.

And so the third sailor was left all alone on the desert island. The wishes of the other two really had come true! The sailor looked at the magic bottle and thought long and hard. Suddenly the cork popped out again and the genie appeared for the third and the last time.

"What is your wish, O great one?" began the genie.
"Well," started the sailor, "since the others wished themselves back home and away from this desert island, well, I've felt a bit lonely."
"Remember," warned the genie, "there is only one wish left!"
"I know," said the sailor, "I just wish I could see them again."

There was a bang, a flash, and suddenly there were the sailor's friends, back with him, all of them stuck on the desert island.

The Hodja and the Poisoned Baklava

TRADITIONAL

Once, when the Hodja was standing in for the village schoolmaster, he was sent a large box of baklava by the parents of one of his students. His mouth watered at the thought of eating them, but he put them away in the drawer of his desk. Shortly afterwards he was called out on urgent business.

He set his students a lot of work to do.

'And I shall expect you to get everything right,' he said, 'or there will be trouble.' He glared at them. 'Big trouble.'

'One thing more,' he said as he made for the door. 'I have enemies. Many enemies. I keep being sent poisoned meats and poisoned sweets. Even,' he added fiercely, 'poisoned baklava. I have to test everything before I eat it. So be warned. If you hope for a long life, don't touch anything that has been sent to me. Especially baklava.'

As soon as he had gone, his nephew, who was one of his students, went to the desk and took out the baklava.

'Don't!' his friends shouted. 'They may be poisoned!'

The boy grinned at them.

'Of course they aren't,' he said. 'He just wants to keep them for himself.' And he started in on the baklava. 'They really are very good,' he said. He ate another one.

When his friends saw that he didn't fall to the floor in a writhing heap they gathered round the Hodja's desk and shared out the baklava.

'But what will we tell him when he finds they've all gone?' one of them said, wiping the crumbs from his mouth.

The Hodja's nephew just smiled.

When the Hodja returned, he went straight to his desk and looked in his drawer. He glared at his students.

'Someone,' he said, 'someone has been at my desk.'

There was silence.

'Someone has been in my drawer.'

Silence.

'And someone has eaten the baklava.'

'I have,' said his nephew.

'*You* have! After what I told you?'

'Yes.'

'Perhaps you have some explanation. If so, I would like to hear it before you die.'

'Well,' said his nephew, 'the work you set was far too hard for me. I couldn't do any of it. Everything I've done is wrong. I knew you would be very angry and my parents would be very disappointed. I felt so ashamed I decided that the only thing to do was to . . . to . . . to put an end to my life. So I ate your poisoned baklava. It was the only way I could think of on the spur of the moment. But the funny thing is, nothing's happened yet. I wonder why that is.'

The Hodja examined his nephew's innocent expression minutely.

'Perhaps,' he said, 'it's just a punishment postponed. In which case I ought to have a look at what work you have done.'

The Hodja and the Poisoned Baklava

The questions in Section A are all about what happens in the story, and what you learn about the different characters in the story.

1 Baklava is a sweet pastry filled with honey and nuts. Write down a line from the story that shows you it was very crumbly.

2 Why did the Hodja put the box of baklava in the drawer of the desk?

3 Why couldn't the Hodja stay and teach the class?

4 What did the Hodja expect the class to do while he was away?

5 **a)** What lie did the Hodja tell the class before he left?
b) Why did he tell the class this lie?

6 Why did the class shout at the Hodja's nephew?

7 What did the Hodja's nephew tell the rest of the class?

8 When did the other students start to believe the Hodja's nephew?

9 What did the students do that shows you they believed him?

10 What was the first thing the Hodja did when he returned to the classroom?

11 **a)** Who else should have owned up as well as the Hodja's nephew?
b) Why do you think they remained silent?

12 What reason did the nephew give for eating the baklava?

13 Why can't the Hodja be cross with his nephew for telling a lie?

14 **a)** Who is your favourite character in this story?
b) What is it you like about this character?

15 Why do you think the Hodja had been sent the baklava in the first place?

The questions in Section B are all about the way in which the writer tells the story.

1 Write down the words used in the first sentence that mean **taking the place of**.

2 Write down the words used in the first paragraph that show you the Hodja was longing to eat the baklava.

3 If someone **glared** at you, what would he be

happy with you   **encouraging you**   **warning you**   **joking with you**

4 Write down one word the writer uses to show how the nephew smiled.

5 Write down the sentence that shows you the nephew had decided what he was going to say to his uncle **before** the Hodja came back into the room.

6 Why, when the Hodja's nephew tells his uncle he has eaten the baklava, do you think the writer puts the word *You* in italics?

7 Why, when the nephew is talking, do you think the writer has used two sets of three dots in this way:
"the only thing to do was to. . . to . . . to put an end to my life."

This story comes from a collection of Funny Stories.

If the baklava **had** been poisoned it would have been a very sad story, but because, right from the beginning, we know that the baklava is **not** poisoned we are never worried about the Hodja's nephew. We know that he is going to be all right.

Imagine how different the story would be if it missed out the first part and began at: "I have enemies. Many enemies. I keep being sent poisoned meats and poisoned sweets." Reading that we might think it was the start of an adventure story.

Turn this story into an adventure story. Start with the words "I have enemies", keep the same characters and the same place and don't let the nephew or the Hodja be poisoned, but write an exciting story in place of a funny one.

Slam and the ghosts

Kevin Crossley-Holland

'Night after night,' said Slam's mother. 'The boor! The great clod-hopper!'

'You can't talk to him without getting angry,' said Douglas. 'You can't even talk about him without getting angry. I'll talk to him.'

'I'll brain him! Bursting in at one o'clock night after night! Blundering about! Leaving his great hoof marks all over the house, the drunkard!'

'I'll talk to him,' said Douglas again.

'I don't know,' said his mother. 'You're so alike—always loyal to each other, always wanting to avoid a scrap. You and Slam, you look the same too.'

'I wonder why,' said Douglas.

'And so unalike . . . You work; you bring home the bacon. And Slam . . .'

'I know,' said Douglas quickly.

'It's the drink,' said Douglas's mother. 'It's wrecking him. Can't you get him off it?'

Secretly, Douglas agreed with his mother. *What Slam really needs*, he thought, *is a bit of a shock.*

Halfway between the pub and their cottage—and it was a couple of miles from one to the other, maybe a bit further—the lane passed under a very steep bank; and at the top of the bank was the old disused graveyard.

That same night, very late, Douglas pulled the white sheet off his bed. He let himself quietly out of the cottage and, under stars sharp as thorns, walked up to the graveyard. There Douglas wrapped the sheet around him and sat down on a gravestone right on top of the bank, overlooking the lane.

'This will cure him,' Douglas said to himself. 'Kill him or cure him. Poor old Slam!'

At much the same time as usual, Slam came staggering up the lane. His shoes were made of lead, and he was singing a wordless song.

When his brother was right beneath him, Douglas stood up and whoo-hooed at him.

'I know!' said Slam, and he added a great hiccup. 'You're the ghost! I know!'

Douglas whoo-hooed again and Slam peered up at the graveyard and tottered sideways.

'Two ghosts!' exclaimed Slam. 'There was only one ghost last night.'

Slowly Douglas turned round, and stared straight into two furious, glaring eyes.

Douglas started back and fell head first over the steep bank. He landed at his brother's feet and broke his neck. Poor old Douglas! That was the end of him.

Slam and the ghosts

The questions in Section A are about what happens in the story and what sort of people the different characters are.

1 Who is Slam's mother talking to at the beginning of the story?

2 Who is Slam's mother talking about at the beginning of the story?

3 Why does Slam come home so late?

4 How is Douglas related to Slam?

5 How are Douglas and Slam similar?

6 How are Douglas and Slam different?

7 Which one of these words do you think describes Douglas best?

drunk   **kind-hearted**   **dangerous**   **selfish**   **angry**

8 What sort of house did Slam live in?

9 What was on top of the steep bank above the lane?

10 What did Douglas take out with him in the middle of the night?

11 What did Douglas do to try and make Slam believe he was a ghost?

12 Why wasn't Slam surprised to see a ghost?

13 Who was surprised by the real ghost?

14 What did surprise Slam?

15 Why did the real ghost look more frightening than Slam's pretend ghost?

16 Why did Douglas think he should frighten Slam?

17 What happened to Douglas in the end?

The questions in Section B are about the way the writer tells the story.

1 Slam's mother uses a great many slang words. What does she mean when she says Slam leaves "his great hoof marks all over the house"?

2 What does Slam's mother mean when she says to Douglas "you bring home the bacon"?

3 Where would Slam's mother hit Slam if she did manage to "brain" him?

4 Why do you think the writer has put the words *"What Slam really needs is a bit of a shock"* in italics.

5 The stars are millions of miles away. What does the writer mean when he says the stars are "as sharp as thorns"?

6 a) When Douglas says "kill him or cure him" what exactly does he think might kill Slam?
   b) What is Douglas trying to "cure" Slam of?

7 Why do you think the song Slam is singing is "wordless"?

8 When the writer says Slam's shoes are "made of lead" what is he telling you about the way Slam was walking?

The story ends very suddenly. Poor Douglas is dead and Slam is left with the ghost! What happens next?
Does Douglas become a real ghost?
The other ghost has tried to frighten Slam before, and failed; what does it do now?
What will Slam do now that he's lost his brother who used to go to work and earn all the money?

Using the same characters continue the story.

Start like this:

Slam dropped his bottle. It smashed into a thousand fragments on the stony lane. Slam didn't notice. He stared at the sight of his brother, wrapped in a white sheet, lying still at the bottom of the steep bank. Then something very strange began to happen.

Why Birds Sing in the Morning

TERRY JONES

 LONG, LONG TIME AGO, before you or I were ever thought of, and before there was any distinction between day and night, the King and Queen of the Light had a baby daughter. She was the most beautiful of all creatures. When she first opened her eyes, they were so bright that they filled the world with light. Everywhere she went, creatures were glad to see her. Plants grew at her touch, and animals would come out of their holes just to sit and watch her go by.

In a cave not far away there lived the Witch of the Dark. She too had an only child – a son. He was a sickly boy, he was always pale and sometimes he grew very thin and had to be nursed back to strength.

One day, however, the old Witch of the Dark brought her son to court and proposed a marriage between him and the Princess. When the King of the Light refused, the old Witch flew into a rage, and that very night she and her son broke into the King's palace and stole the beautiful Princess. They took her and locked her up in a dark cave on the other side of the mountains, and there she stayed for a long time. She cried and cried, but it was no good. The Witch would not let the Princess out until she agreed to marry her son.

Meanwhile the animals went to the King and said: 'Where is your daughter? When she is away from us all the world is dark. The plants do not grow and many of us have nothing to eat.'

The King of the Light told the animals what had happened, and the animals all agreed that they would help him look for his daughter.

So the lions and tigers went into the jungle and searched there. The rabbits and moles looked under the earth, and the fish and the turtles searched the seas, but none of them could find any trace of her. Meanwhile the birds were looking in the air and treetops, and the eagle flew off into the mountains. It flew up and up, until it was flying over their very summits. Still it flew on, over the other side and down into a region where it had never been before.

At length, the eagle grew tired and was forced to rest amongst some rocks. He hadn't been there long, however, before he heard a beautiful voice singing a sad song. Immediately he recognized it was the Princess, and he called out to her. But the eagle had only a raucous screech for a voice, and the Princess thought it was the old Witch returning. So she stopped her singing and would not make another sound. The eagle sat there, wondering what to do, when all at once he saw a black speck in the sky. It was the Witch's son, coming to visit the Princess on his mother's broomstick.

The eagle hid, and watched as the Witch's son rolled aside the great stone at the entrance of the cave. Immediately a great brightness flooded out from the cave, as the beautiful Princess came out, and filled everywhere with light. But she had tears in her eyes, and a rainbow shone all around her.

'Ah!' cried the Witch's son. 'I'm tired of waiting!' And he took hold of the beautiful girl, and threw her on the ground. Whereupon the eagle swooped down on them, snapping his beak fiercely at the Witch's son, and lifted the Princess up on his back. The Witch's son grabbed his mother's broomstick, and started hitting out at the eagle. By accident, however, he struck the Princess a blow on the side of her head, so hard that the broomstick broke in two. But the Princess held tight to the eagle, and they soared up into the sky.

The eagle carried the Princess back across the mountains, and wherever they flew they lit up the world that had been lying dark for so long. And the Witch's son got on the broomstick and followed after them. But because the broomstick was broken, he could never quite catch up with them. At length, however, the eagle had to rest again. He let the Princess down off his back and told her to hide, promising to wake her up as soon as the Witch's son had gone past.

So the Princess hid in a cave, and the world went dark once more while the Witch's pale son flew past in the sky. When he had gone, the eagle tried to wake the Princess up, but the blow from the broomstick had made her a bit deaf, and even the eagle with his raucous voice could not wake her. So the eagle asked some sparrows to help him, and they all made as much noise as they could, but still the Princess did not wake up. Eventually the eagle went round all the birds in the neighbourhood and got them all to make as much noise as possible. Finally the Princess awoke, and came out of the cave, lighting the world as she did so.

'Quick!' said the eagle. 'Get on my back – we must be off before the Witch's son comes past again on his broomstick.' So the Princess got on his back again and away they flew, bringing light to the world wherever they went.

And so they continue to this day, for the Princess and the eagle were turned into the sun, and still they ride high up in the sky; and the Witch's son was turned into the moon. And at the end of every day, when the eagle has to rest, the Princess hides while the Witch's son goes past – and if you look up at the moon, you can still see him with his mother's broken broomstick over his shoulder. The Princess is still as beautiful as ever, now she is the sun, but she is also a little deaf, and that is why all the birds sing as hard as they can every morning in order to wake her up.

Why Birds Sing in the Morning

The questions in this section are all about what happens in the first part of the story.

1 What was unusual about the eyes of the Princess?

2 What happened to the plants when the Princess touched them?

3 At the start of the story what does the Witch want the Princess to do?

4 Why does the Witch become very angry?

5 What does the Witch think will happen if she locks up the Princess?

6 Write down the words from the story that show the Princess was very upset to be locked up by the Witch.

7 **a)** What happened to the plants when the Princess was away?
   b) How did this affect the animals?

8 How did the animals decide to help the King and the Queen?

9 How can you tell from the story that the eagle was a very strong bird?

10 Why was it a mistake for the eagle to call out to the Princess?

11 What do you think the eagle would have done if it hadn't called out?

12 What method of transport was used by the Witch's son?

13 How can you tell from the story that the eagle had excellent eyesight?

14 Why couldn't the Princess escape from the cave?

15 Explain clearly what made the rainbow around the Princess.

16 Why was it lucky that the eagle was near to the cave?

17 Why did the broomstick break?

18 What did the eagle use as a weapon?

The questions in this section are all about what happens at the end of the story.

1 a) Why did the Earth suddenly light up again?
  b) What was the Princess doing when, once again, the Earth went dark?

2 What do you think would have happened if the Witch's son **hadn't** broken the broomstick?

3 How did the eagle carry the Princess?

4 What do you think the eagle did while the Princess was hiding? (Read the passage very carefully before you decide on your answer).

5 The writer says the eagle has a **raucous** voice. What do you think **raucous** means?

6 Why did the eagle have to ask the sparrows for help?

7 If you read the second paragraph again it says that sometimes the Witch's son "grew very thin". Remember what the son turns into and then explain why the writer wrote this about the Witch's son.

8 a) Do you like this story?
  b) If your answer is "Yes" say why you enjoyed reading it.
    If your answer is "No" explain why you didn't like reading it.

This story is rather like a **myth**. **Myths** are usually stories from ancient civilisations that tell how the Earth was created and how the ancient gods and heroes had extraordinary adventures on their new world. This story is like that in many ways, except that it was written quite recently. The writer has made up a myth he would like to believe in.

Make up a **myth** of your own.

Make up a **myth** that explains why every week is divided up into 7 days. Were the days shared out among seven sisters, seven dwarves, seven gods, seven spirits, seven different workers or was it seven different animals?

How did the different days get their names?
Why is the first day called **Sun**day?
What happened on the sixth day that made people call it **Fri**day?

Explain it all in your **Myth**.

Everest

Hillary

Tensing

The only way to climb the mountain was to attempt it in stages. They had to set up camp after camp, each higher than the one before. The last camp had to be close enough to the top for the climbers to reach the summit and return safely in a day.

The first problem was to find a way up the icefall. Edmund Hillary led a party to do this. They picked their way among ice boulders and tottering ice pillars. They crossed, or dodged round, gaping crevasses and they scaled ice cliffs. All the time, the ice groaned and grumbled. They named various places – Mike's Horror, Hillary's Horror, Hell Fire Alley, Atom Bomb Area and Ghastly Crevasse. But in the end, they reached the cwm. Getting back to camp was unpleasant, but now it had been climbed once, the icefall did not seem to be so terrible after all.

Some members of the party then made the path as easy as they could. They bridged crevasses with wooden planks, they chopped steps, they fixed ropes to the sides of cliffs, and, at one point, they hung a rope ladder. They also marked the path with flags. The movement of the glacier and fresh falls of snow kept spoiling their work, but the Sherpas were able to carry load after load of supplies into the Western Cwm. Here they set up their advanced camp.

The next step was to find a way up the sheer wall of the Lhotse face. After several days they managed this and again they prepared the way with fixed ropes and steps. Not surprisingly, it was hard to persuade some of the Sherpas to carry their loads up there. But on May 21st, they finally pitched Camp 8 on the South Col.

Hunt had chosen two assault teams for the final attack. The first was Charles Evans and Tom Bourdillon; the other was Edmund Hillary and Tensing. On May 26th, Evans and Bourdillon set out. At first all went well, and the men below watched them with excitement. Only Tensing was silent. He thought a Sherpa should be one of the first men to climb to the top. By one o'clock Evans and Bourdillon had reached the South Summit. They could now see the very peak of the mountain and it was only 400 yards away. Should they go on? Unfortunately they were already tired and they were fast running out of oxygen. Probably they could have reached the top, but they knew that if they did so they would die on their way back down. At six o'clock they staggered into Camp 8, barely able to walk, with their faces covered in frost. It was now the turn of Hillary and Tensing.

On May 27th the weather was so bad they could do nothing. But on the following day they set out. Three other men came with them to carry their tent, spare oxygen and food. The five men climbed until mid-afternoon and then looked for a place to camp. The slopes were so steep that it seemed impossible to find one, but in the end they discovered a ledge, a tiny shelf on the face of a precipice, thousands of feet high. The three companions turned back, leaving the equipment they had carried, including a large cylinder of oxygen. This was the supply Hillary and Tensing needed for the night. It is impossible to sleep at that height without oxygen.

The ledge had a slope of 30 degrees, so Hillary and Tensing levelled it as well as they could, prising rocks out of the frozen ground. The ground was too hard

climbers on Everest

a high camp on Everest

for tent pegs, so they stuck oxygen bottles in the snow and used those. When they had put the tent up they had supper of soup, sardines on biscuits, dates and pint after pint of sweet lemonade. They also ate a tin of apricots which Hillary had kept hidden until then. It was a great treat.

The night was miserable. Every now and then a gust of wind threatened to blow them off their ledge. They also found that one of their helpers had taken back the adaptor for the large bottle of oxygen. They only dared use their climbing oxygen for four hours, so they had little sleep.

At 6.30 the next morning they set off. It was a hard struggle to reach the South Summit, and after that came the dreadful ridge that had defeated Bourdillon and Evans. The only way was to chip steps all the way up it. They went over one hump after another, hoping each would be the last, but the ridge seemed to go on for ever. At one point they reached a sheer wall forty feet high. It looked impossible, but it had a crack in it and they were able to force their way up that. At 11.30 a.m. they finally reached the summit.

What do you do at the top of Everest? Hillary and Tensing shook hands, like the English, then hugged one another like Sherpas. Tensing buried a few sweets and chocolates as an offering to the gods that live on the mountain, and Hillary buried a little white crucifix. Hillary next took some photographs of the mountains all around, then three of Tensing. There is no photograph of Hillary on the summit because Tensing did not know how to use a camera and Hillary thought it was hardly the time to teach him. After a quarter of an hour they made their way down. They reached the South Col by the evening, just as the oxygen ran out. The following morning they arrived in the Western Cwm, so all

Tensing on the summit

they had to do was to go down the icefall for the last time and make the long hike through Nepal.

The expedition had been a great success, and everyone had shown tremendous skill and courage. Both Hunt and Hillary were knighted. But why had they wanted to reach the top of Everest in the first place? The only answer Sir John Hunt could give was, 'We climbed it because it was there.'

Because it's there!

1 What did the climbers make at every stage up the mountain?

2 Who led the party that found a way through the icefall?

3 The climbers gave names to different parts of the icefall. Look at the names carefully. How do you think the climbers were feeling when they made up these names?

4 Once a way had been found through the icefall, what was the next job that had to be done?

5 The third paragraph tells you how the climbers dealt with crevasses. The way they dealt with the crevasses should give you a clue as to what a crevasse is. What do you think a crevasse is?

6 What were the flags for?

7 Who used the path and what did they use it for?

8 What was the number of the last camp?

9 Why do you think the Sherpas didn't want to carry their loads up the Lhotse face?

10 Camp 8 was set up on May 21st. It was May 26th before the climbers set out for the top. Why do you think they waited for those five days?

11 What were the names of the two men who were supposed to reach the top of the mountain first?

12 What were the names of the two men who did reach the top first?

13 On what date did the men who did reach the top set out?

14 How can you tell that there was hardly any air for people to breathe at the top of Mount Everest?

15 Why do you think Hillary and Tensing didn't carry their own tent and their own spare oxygen?

1 a) What was the problem Hillary and Tensing had when they tried to put up their tent?

   b) Explain how they solved this problem.

2 a) What was the problem Hillary and Tensing had when they tried to go to sleep?

   b) Why couldn't they solve this problem?

3 Tensing was a Sherpa. Why do you think Tensing was particularly pleased to be one of the first men to the top? (If you read the fifth paragraph again you will find a clue to help you with your answer).

4 Why are there only pictures of Tensing on the top of Mount Everest?

5 How did Tensing react differently to Hillary when they reached the top of Mount Everest?

6 In the last paragraph we are told that Edmund Hillary was rewarded for being the first person to reach the top of Mount Everest by being knighted, he became **Sir** Edmund Hillary. Another man is mentioned in the same paragraph. His name is Sir John Hunt. He didn't reach the top of Everest. What do you think he did to be rewarded in this way?

The **account** you have just read on the first ascent of Mount Everest sets out the facts in **chronological** order. **Chronological** order means that you are told about the different events in the order that they happened.

Because it is a detailed account it contains not only **times** and **dates**, but also the **names** of many of the different parts of the mountain. There are also many details about how the climbers managed to get over different parts of the mountain.

Using all this information make a large **map** of the mountain with **labels** showing **where** the following places were and **when** the different climbers arrived there.

You should try to include all the following places:

The icefall with Mike's Horror and Hillary's Horror and Ghastly Crevasse.

The Western Cwm.	The South Summit.
The Lhotse face.	The Ridge.
Camp 8.	The sheer wall.
The South Col.	The Top.
The camp on the ledge.	

Sources

The texts used in this book are extracted from the following full sources, and we are grateful for their permission to reproduce copyright material.

p 4   From *Call 999* by Sylvia Moody, *Front Page Story* by Roger Stevens and *Pet Squad* by Paul Shipton, all TREETOPS series (OUP 1995), reproduced by permission of Oxford University Press.

p 6   From *The Year I was Born, 1981*, text by Sally Tagholm, illustrations by Michael Evans (Signpost Books, 1989), reproduced by permission of the publishers.

p 8   From *A Nursery Companion* by Peter and Iona Opie (OUP, 1980) reproduced by permission of Oxford University Press.

p 10   From *The Oxford Illustrated Junior Dictionary* (OUP, 1989), reproduced by permission of Oxford University Press.

p 12   From *The Oxford Children's Picture Book of Living Things* by Susan Goodman (OUP, 1993), reproduced by permission of Oxford University Press.

p 14   From *The Oxford Children's Pocket Book of Knowledge* (OUP, 1992), reproduced by permission of Oxford University Press.

p 16   From *The Oxford Children's A–Z of Geography* by Dick Bateman (OUP, 1996), reproduced by permission of Oxford University Press. Photographs reproduced by permission of Rex Features.

p 18   From *The Oxford Children's Book of Science* by Charles Taylor and Stephen Pople (OUP, 1984), reproduced by permission of Oxford University Press. Photographs reproduced by permission of Oxford Scientific Films.

p 20   From *Clothes* by J Drum and H Sutton (Heritage Books/BBC, 1986)

p 22   From *The Oxford Children's A–Z of Technology* by Robin Kerrod (OUP, 1996), reproduced by permission of Oxford University Press. Photographs reproduced by permission of the Science Photo Library.

p 24   Text from *What is Art?* by Rosemary Davidson (OUP, 1993), used by permission of Cynthia Parzych Publishing, Inc. PHD656 'Monet in his Floating Studio', 1874 by Edouard Manet (1932–83), Neue Pinakothek, Munich/ Bridgeman Art Library, London; and BAL5610 'The Beach at Trouville' 1870 by Claude Monet (1840–1926), National Gallery, London/ Bridgeman Art Library, London, reproduced by permission of the Bridgeman Art Library; detail from 'The Beach at Trouville' by Claude Monet reproduced by courtesy of the Trustees, The National Gallery, London.

p 26   'A Small Dragon' by Brian Patten, Copyright © Brian Patten 1969, reproduced by permission of the author c/o Rogers, Coleridge & White Ltd, 20 Powis Mews, London W11 1JN. Illustrated page from Michael Harrison and Christopher

Stuart-Clark (eds): *The Oxford Treasury of Classic Poems* (OUP, 1996), reproduced by permission of Oxford University Press.

p 28   'Four Children, One Being, Four Children, One Seeing' by Julie Holder, first published in John Foster (ed): *Spaceways* (OUP, 1986), text reproduced by permission of the author, illustrated page reproduced by permission of Oxford University Press.

p 32   'Posting Letters' by Gregory Harrison from *Posting Letters* (OUP, 1968), Copyright © Gregory Harrison 1968, reproduced by permission of the author. Illustrated page from John Foster (ed): *A Fourth Poetry Book* (OUP, 1982), reproduced by permission of Oxford University Press.

p 36   'The Pardoner's Tale' from Oxford Junior History Book 2 by Roy Burrell (OUP, 1980), reproduced by permission of Oxford University Press.

p 40   'Bro Tiger Goes Dead' from *Anancy-Spiderman*, text © 1988 by James Berry, reproduced by permission of Walker Books Ltd, London. Illustrated page from Michael Harrison and Christopher Stuart Clarke (eds): *The Oxford Treasury of Children's Stories* (OUP, 1994), reproduced by permission of Oxford University Press.

p 44   'Like Dog, Like Dad' by W K McNeil from *Ozark Mountain Humor* (August House, 1989). Illustrated page from Dennis Pepper (ed): *The Oxford Funny Story Book* (OUP, 1996), reproduced by permission of Oxford University Press.

p 48   'The Hodja and the Poisoned Baklava', traditional story from W K McNeil (ed): *Ozark Mountain Humor* (August House, 1989). Illustrated page from Dennis Pepper (ed): *The Oxford Funny Story Book* (OUP, 1996), reproduced by permission of Oxford University Press.

p 52   'Slam and the Ghosts' by Kevin Crossley-Holland from *British Folk Tales* (Orchard Books, 1987). Illustrated page from Dennis Pepper (ed): *The Oxford Book of Scary Tales* (OUP, 1992), reproduced by permission of Oxford University Press.

p 56   Text from *Fairy Tales* by Terry Jones, illustrations by Michael Foreman, reproduced by permission of Pavilion Books.

p 60   From *The Oxford Children's History* Book 2 by Peter and Mary Speed (OUP, 1983), reproduced by permission of Oxford University Press.